hannah k

how
i've
loved
before

how i've loved before

how
i've
loved
before

hannah kim

*for all the cynical hopeless romantics,
may we find the balance we need*

how i've loved before

sat on the miss-matched floor
i collected snails from around the garden
to bring them home
back to their family
i didn't understand
that snails were meant to roam free

or that one day i'd choose **freedom** too

hannah kim

running home from school
in the rain
hand in hand
our feet soaked through
walked through the door
the heating hit like summer
warming our shivering bones
we curled up on the sofa
hot chocolate in hand
slippers toasting our feet
like marshmallows

those are the days i miss the most

coming home from nan's
my stomach full
with the greasy chicken
and parsnips
i don't eat anymore
i'd climb into your bed
with the teddies and magazines
we'd watch
home is where the heart is
and i'd snuggle up next to you
knowing nothing could make me blue

those are the days i miss the most

how i've loved before

there are pictures of us
in a box at my mother's house
dust covered
in the corner of the loft
there are memories of you
in my mind
all sepia toned

the blow up pool
we filled with bubblegum
the way i always thought
you'd be the one
the summer's day
carrier bags hanging on the door
your top bunk
you showed me more

chocolate mousses
in the middle of the night
you slept with your socks on
i never knew why
in the garden
we had a house of our own
carpet laid on the grass
i was home

i climbed the tree in your garden
higher than where your cousin got stuck
i squeezed through your kitchen window
when we were locked out
i'd stay on the phone for hours with you
i don't know what we talked about
but it was important to us
we made mud potions and love potions
just hoping it'd be enough
always going to the places
we were never meant to go
we'd do each others makeup
and put on a show
just me and you in your room
singing our favourite songs
you always hated that my hair
stayed crimped way longer than yours
being squished in the back seat
going on holiday together
wearing our matching outfits
so everyone would ask
if we were twins
now you have twins

how i've loved before

sunday morning
a bag full of recyclables
we walked past the park
in-between the bungalows
with crooked roof tiles
over the uneven pavement
with the grass growing through
past the holly bush
to the same old shop
where'd you buy papers
that i'd pretend to read

if i closed my eyes
i could walk all the way back
with just the sun beating down
to guide me
to the house where we would
mow the grass together
check your wellies for spiders
dip my biscuits
till they fell into your tea
build the furniture twice
because we'd always
get something wrong

but we always fixed it
because **we were a team**

hannah kim

sharing oranges with you
is my favourite thing to do
you said i'm real good at the dusting
so now it's my weekend job
you put on dolly
and i dance until i'm out of breath
we tend the garden wearing our hats
you know my favourite flowers are peonies
i try to count your ornaments
but there's way too many cats
i tell you all the food i've eaten
and you are so proud
you watch the shows too scary for me
and **i fall asleep with my head on your lap**

how i've loved before

he was never a morning person
only i could wake him up
he'd drink his coffee from my cup
that he claimed was his
he'd teach me guitar
and we'd sing our song
now it doesn't matter where i am
when i hear the melody
i'll be encapsulated in a moment
that i never wanted to end

my first bad boy
the first to never understand

not sure what i liked the most
the attention or you

we kissed on the grass
and i went home singing
"rome wasn't built in a day"
like we were **bigger than the roman empire**

how i've loved before

i never understood
why you'd ever want me at all

you told me years later
you saw me help your little sister
and make sure she didn't fall

i can still remember your smile
before searing honesty left your lips

even if we only lasted a minute
it was worthwhile

and i'll never forget that
when i look up

death in the family
i died too
dyed my hair black
wishing i was somebody new
that's when you wanted
to be friends with the ugly side of me
we walked in the dark
miles for the sake of it
i didn't know if i'd make it home again
i met your grandma
and drew you a picture
you pinned to your wall
i told you i loved you
then left **when the sugar turned bitter**

how i've loved before

i
had
wanted
you
for
so
long
but
i
couldn't
kiss
you
no
then
we'd
be
c u r s e d
and
you'd
be
long
gone

when all the words that they told us held faith
didn't hold up their end of the bargain
i found myself lost in the world
what happens to love when i'm dissipating
and you're shelved in a box
does it fall into the wrong hands?
ones that distract me
from the worst pain i've ever felt
do the empty wine bottles line up
until they are taken to the bank
or do they shatter on the floor
part of me has always liked the way
my broken pieces glisten

you don't remember
when you first kissed me
but it was on the steps behind the shops
we had sugar on our lips
from the doughnuts we were eating

i don't remember
the end of the movie
but you made me feel so comfortable
i never would've guessed how
you never felt safe at home

maybe she remembers
the way you'd look at her
best friends for a reason that's for sure
and if i didn't know better
i would've guessed you'd still be together

i watched you love a boy
who would never love you like i could
i watched you dancing
you didn't know how much i wanted to
dance with you

i held your hand
climbed to the top of the world with you
stayed out late
because you never wanted to go home
and neither did i

put your pictures
in my sketchbook to keep forever
then you disappeared
like the hair slides i could never buy enough of
but i couldn't replace you

we were laughing
and smiling
your mum
was the kindest
we were friends
with all the love
of nothing more
just holding hands
trusting
kicking your shoes
out the window
watching films
in your bed
and talking
about the world
do you remember me saying
i never stayed for too long

the ad in the newspaper and your persistence
the friends that i wanted to kiss but didn't
your family and it's ludicrousness
the tunnel on the way home
your heart in my hands
the pain that you gave me
returned to sender
maybe my timing could have been better
than when your life was on its hinges
my clothes in a bag and my lies to get you there
flashes of kissing someone else in my head
i was all that you had
and **your love was wasted on me**

how i've loved before

they say the third time's the charm
that's how many times it took
to not love you
your electricity in my bones
slowly killing me with the want of something more
you took my friend to the cinema
but never me
swore that you loved me
i was blind as can be
finishing my sentences
like you knew me

i bought the cds you played in your room
to feel closer to you
i wanted to understand
why you never followed through
but i realised you were an equation
all the mathematicians in the world
could never figure out
i could never figure you out
but hell
i wanted to

how much of a fool was i for loving you again
still can't watch that movie without you
that chocolate still tastes like your lips
i don't know why
i thought you'd show
when an excuse was imminent
instead you showed me
you didn't need to know a lot
to pretend to love someone
and that's how i learned
i could never count on you

unspoken
only we knew
we slept in my single bed
maybe i dreamt it
or maybe that's why she was angry
all those months before
but our lips pressed against each other's
my hands traced her body
and in the morning
we never said
a thing
time flew away from us
but my heart could have felt so much

if we were brave enough to not leave the words
unspoken

how i've loved before

your mum hated me and all our
extracurricular activities
i baked you cookies
and got to school early
i watched all the shows
you thought were funny
i walked to the party
where you told me you loved me
i felt the kind of happiness
you could only feel from something hollow
i wonder when you took down
the photo from your wall
the one you always swore was innocent

you'd always cheat at every game
couldn't bare losing to me
so i learned to cheat better at every game
i had to win
if you were my biggest competition
i knew i could go anywhere

but somewhere along the way
you stopped playing the game

how i've loved before

the sky poured its heart out that night
as we sat on the paving slabs
you told me about the girl you missed
but you always came back to me

in your room we kissed
you wanted to forget all the pain
for a moment i thought you were it all
that the only thing i had left was us

now my mind fills the night up
with all this hate
how did we get so fucked up
when i still remember you
wrapping me up in your jacket
and walking me home safe

but we both know
there's no such thing as a safe

hannah kim

you came in like a crashing sea
full disclosure
you were never good for me
i thought you had the world figured out
but you were drinking in the park
walking me to your house
to the room you shared with your brother

even the best captains lose control
i know that
the sea's a beast that has no soul
i was lost with no way out
wanting to trust someone
how crazy was that
i was floating with the yellow roses

i never played you the song i wrote for you
but **it still gets stuck in my head**

how i've loved before

words meant more from your lips
i shared everything
nothing left to spare
i took your card of chance and held it close to my
heart
you took mine and flew it far away
one troubled soul and one saviour
our paths paralleled each other
close to meeting
but they never crossed
we missed each other by a matter of moments
now i think back to what could have been
if only i had gone off course
we'd be sitting in a field
like we used to talk about
sharing our dreams and making new memories
but i'll never kiss you on the lips
instead i'll dream about the love that
almost was

i've
never
held
on
to
the
right
people

to
the
ones
that
made
me
feel
tall

how i've loved before

there's dead flowers
decorating my windowsill
i've become attached to their fragile petals
that crisp with a delicate touch

their death draws me in
like some kind of dark entity
i find their frail existence beautiful

it always has to end

you held my head up
with your hands
so i could see the movie
i wore your jumper
and called it mine
i saw you wear it
the other day

you walked me
along the beach
and pulled out
an artificial rose
it's still packed up
in the boxes
ready for when i move

you told me
i was your sunshine
yet the tide
was always out
you hated how
i was someone before you

so i rewrote my history
to please you
because i was warm
in your jumper
and i was safe
in your hands
or so you made me believe

when i got home

i realised i still had your jumper on

now it's resting on my sofa

the blue wool blend

that took away the chill of the british summer

i can't help but to think

how many times i would have been

saved by your jumper

if you had never left

it's been more than a year
but i picked the phone up anyway
now i'm sitting here
in the home that you made
i'll make my own coffee
in the same cup i have at home
i pick up the guitar
but your eyes
they're not dry anymore
you say you always want to see me
so why didn't you call?

how i've loved before

you and i
have our own
little club

take my hand
it's us
against the world

we're a force
to be
reckoned with

a team
stronger than
no other

you're my world
my life
my everything

and i'll
never
let you go

no matter
how old
we grow

i'll buy you flowers
every week if i have to
to show you how much you're worth
and i'll apologise when i'm in the wrong
i never want to leave the blame on you
i'll teach you all i know
so you'll never be helpless
i'll squeeze your hand
to tell you i love you
i'll do anything
for you

how i've loved before

she was sweet
like her coffee
after way too much sugar
i would leave my house
in the morning
ride the bus
to sit in the coffee shop
and we'd talk about
our failing relationships
she'd say
we should run away together
and that's all i wanted
for her to look at the me
the way she would somebody new

we drank wine on the bench
outside the pub
"buckle up"
i told myself
she told me all the ways
he was her perfect teammate
and i couldn't be happy for her
so my green eyes turned into white lies
like they did all those years ago
sat on the pavement
outside the party
convincing her
he was never good enough
so i could keep her to myself

everything felt so familiar
did our souls meet before?
did divine intervention call
and say "this one's for you"

were we meant to fall apart
like everything eventually does
we never needed to see the view
because we both already knew

my mirrored armour wasn't fooling you
you could see straight through me
and i couldn't let you watch me
fall in love with you

and like the new year's resolutions
those promises you made to me
they were never going to stick
and like that **you fell away from me**

how i've loved before

good things take time
and i have always been so impatient

but with you
i wanted to take a breath
and feel the air in my lungs
before i rushed down another
and life moved on

in his room
in his arms
in his bed
there were words
left unsaid
and i was trying
but i couldn't
get out of my head

put my top back on
and my walls hit him
faster than a mustang
he asked
"why?"
but what the hell could i say?
"my soul has been broken before
and i'm just trying to make sure i'm safe
you know i trust you
but i trusted him too"

how fucked up would it be for you
to watch me let you in
and fall in deep
to then leave?

oh wait

you did

i'll forget the smiles between kisses
the way your hand guided my back
i'll forget the little hi's
that used to get me by
the hand holding in the car
and the sight of you
smoking out your window at 3am
but you'll still have my name on your skin
in **permanent ink**

the lights lit up the dark
like stars in the sky
and we were in heaven above it all
we couldn't see a thing
but the beat pulsed through our bodies
all the nights where we
would cry ourselves to sleep
all the nights where we
drank together to forget
all the frantic phone calls
and SOS messages
sent to and fro
came together
and tied themselves into a knot
because we were screaming
at the top of our lungs
singing the songs
that got us through our pain
together
we were on top of the world
alone together
but for once nothing else mattered
and **i wouldn't want to be there
with anyone else but you**

how can he look like an angel

with those blue green eyes?

how can he look at me

like that?

how can he feel the same way about himself that
i do?

has he never let anyone dig deeper? has he just
left before they could? left himself in the dark?
unrooted himself from everyone because he was
scared they'd see straight through him?

because if so...

me too

how i've loved before

the lights
hit the water
like the milk
in my coffee
whilst the radio played
i admired
all your books
like a
curious collector
and **you were**
a character
i'd written
years ago

there we were

laying face to face on his sofa

my heart heavy with my past experiences

playing over and over

i'd been taken away

by distraction with him

but all the laughter in the world

couldn't cure me

his fingertips ran

up and down

the curve of my side

as i laid there

in his company

he asked if i was okay

but i couldn't answer

i can never answer

how i've loved before

i wish i had
a childlike
gaze of love

jumping in
the deep end
with no armbands on

making daisy chains
without considering
how long they last

enjoying the moment
like it will go on forever
no questions asked

i can pinpoint
the exact moment my heart broke
drinking wine in the bar garden
with two guys all over me
and all i could think about was you
saying **she was god damn pretty**

doodles on the napkin
you knew it was too cold for your outfit
when you left the house
we sat scoring all the strangers
but for each other we only show love
you support me in the best way
give me more than i deserve
all i want to is to protect you
so you never get hurt
but **we can't take each other's pain away**
we can only sit in it together

i gave you everything i had in me
riddled myself with anxiety
i gave you my armour
but you threw it into the sea
is this what i get for loving someone?

to have my pennies stolen
my wishes never stood a chance
i just wanted to feel whole again
you never understood that
we were building bonfires
just to **watch it all burn down**

how i've loved before

let me be the first
to hold your hand
in the dark

no secret
you can tell me
will be too heavy

no scars
will disfigure
the way i look at you

it's okay if we don't
leave together
as long as
i have you right now

close my eyes
and pretend you're here

but you're not

hold my breath
until i'm blue

i'm blue

cut you off
to save myself

i think it might be too late

wait another seven years
and say

"it's been too long"

how i've loved before

run my fingertips
over his tattoos
they'll never be yours

run my fingers
through his hair
he'll never be you

i can't think
about it anymore
it hurts just to breathe

i can't dream
about it anymore
it hurts knowing you're gone

here i am
on my own
crying on my sofa
where you once held me tight

here i am
all alone
and i know things
are never going to feel right

hannah kim

if i follow the moon
will it just take me
to the ghost of you?
past the closed candy floss stalls
back to the empty shores
and the sleeping boats

just a ghost town now
do you remember when
the lights were too bright?
the fireworks in the dark
rain flooding from the sky
just you and i

i hugged you to keep you warm
we ran to your car
put the heating on full
i tried to distract you
got you talking
about your favourite music
i still listen to that song

pin my hair back
out of my face
make the same hot chocolate
from years ago
climb under the blankets
like they're my fort
watch the same shows
i would watch
staying home from school
collect my pennies in a pot
saving all my wishes for me
burn candles that smell
of my nan's peonies
watch the rain
from my back door
take my socks off
in the middle of the night
spend an hour
cooking my favourite meal
fill the vase on my windowsill
with flowers for my one love
sit on the footpath
watching the sea
drive down the back roads
to the places i don't know
scrunch my nose with laughter
at my own jokes
make daisy chains
in my mum's garden
turn up the music
on the way home
pick up my guitar
and sing my heart out to
how i've loved before

how i've loved before

*when i was younger, i found love in the people
close to me; loving my mother was comfort,
loving my nan was helping each other, loving my
grandad was learning, loving my uncle was
having a partner in crime, loving my brother was
a power struggle, loving my best friend was
having adventures, loving my childhood
sweetheart was being cared for.*

*as i grew up their love fell away from me and i
found comfort in anyone i could, despite whether
they were good for me or whether i was good for
them. that's when i loved for safety.*

*as a mother, i found a new territory of love that is
unconditional, overwhelming and life-changing.
to me it was important that i taught my daughter
to love herself and that's where i drew a blank.
all the years i had been focusing on the love i
found in other people, that i had neglected to find
the love for myself and i knew i had to change
that.*

*now i find; comfort from my mother, strength
from my daughter, a bookmark from my
strawberry, bubble wrap from my best friend, and
love for myself.*

Printed in Great Britain
by Amazon